Home Life

Neil Tonge

WAYLAND

First published in 2008 by Wayland

This paperback edition published in 2010 by Wayland

Reprinted in 2010 by Wayland

Copyright © Wayland 2008

Wayland
338 Euston Road
London NW1 3BH

Wayland Australia
Level 17/207 Kent Street
Sydney, NSW 2000

Editor: Katie Powell
Consultant: Stewart Ross
Designer: Phipps Design

British Library Cataloguing in Publication Data

Tonge, Neil
Home life. - (Britain since 1948)
1. Family - Great Britain - History - 20th century - Juvenile literature
2. Social change - Great Britain - History - 20th century - Juvenile literature
3. Great Britain - Social conditions - 20th century - Juvenile literature
I. Title
306.8'5'0941'09045

ISBN 978 0 7502 6362 7

Printed in China

Wayland is a division of Hachette Children's Books, an Hachette UK company,
www.hachette.co.uk

Picture acknowledgements: Advertising Archives: 8, 16, 21, 22, © Airbus
2008: 23, Peter Anderson/DK/Getty Images: 10, Barnaby's Studios/Mary
Evans PL: 14, 24, Corbis: front cover, 9, Clive Dixon/Rex Features: 12, Michael
Dunley/Rex Features: 29, Foliofoto: 7, Leeds Archives: front cover, 4, Ina
Peters/Istockphoto: 15, Picturepoint/Topham: 5, Pixland/Corbis: 25,
Popperfoto: 26, Stu Salmon/IStockphoto: 11, Topfoto: 6, 19,
© Universal/Kobal Collection: 20, Wayland: 17, 27, 28.

Thank you to One Plus One for the use of the reference on p13: Reynolds, J., &
Mansfield, P. (1999). The effect of changing attitudes to marriage on its
stability. In J. Simons (ed.). High divorce rates:
The state of the evidence on reasons and remedies. London: Lord
Chancellor's Department.

Contents

Britain in 1948   4

How Homes have Changed   6

Looking After the Home   8

Furnishing the Home   10

Changes in Family Life   12

Childhood   14

The Car   16

Radio and Television   18

The Cinema   20

Family Holidays   22

Changes in Food   24

Shops and Shopping   26

A Multicultural Society   28

Timeline   30

Glossary and Further Information   31

Index   32

Words in **bold** can be found in the glossary.

Britain in 1948

From 1939 to 1945, Britain fought a long and exhausting war. The cost in lives was enormous, with almost 450,000 people killed and over 1 million injured. In addition, 0.5 million houses were made unfit for habitation due to German bombing raids. But the British people were determined to rebuild their country, and the Labour government that swept into power in 1945 promised better living conditions.

Building a New Britain

The task of building new homes and improving people's living conditions was a daunting one. New houses had to be rebuilt to replace those destroyed in the war and vast areas of decaying Victorian slums in the inner cities also had to be cleared. In these slums it was common for several families to share a single toilet and gas cooker. Mice and rats were everywhere, and families were often infested with **fleas** and **scabies**.

Voices from history

'There were six in my family and our house was a *"two-up, two-down"*. A coal fire was burning in the grate, winter and summer. It was our only source of heat and only means of cooking and boiling water. We had an earth toilet outside in the stone-flagged courtyard, which we shared with our neighbours. We got our water from an outside tap.'

Memories of John Blackthorne, living in a Yorkshire mill town in the late 1940s.

▲
Slum interior • The basement of a 'back-to-back' terraced house in Leeds in the 1950s being used as a bathroom.

TIMELINE

1945	The end of the Second World War
1945	A Labour government comes to power, led by Clement Atlee
1946	Children begin to be given milk each day
1948	The National Health Service is formed

Working-class families that didn't rent a council house from the local authority lived in a typical 'two-up, two-down'. This usually had two bedrooms on the first floor and two rooms on the ground floor. There was a tiny scullery or kitchen at the back, opening out on to a yard with an outside toilet.

Improving Lives

Clement Attlee's Labour government began tackling poverty by improving the health of the nation. In 1948, the National Health Service (NHS) was set up, providing free medical and dental care for everyone. From 1946 onwards, school children were given a third of a pint of milk at school every day. Young children and pregnant women continued to be given free orange juice and cod liver oil after the war, too. **Inoculation** and **vaccination** against diseases such as **measles** and **whooping cough** dramatically reduced the death rate by a third.

Labour's election poster • *Despite the admiration for Britain's wartime Conservative leader, Winston Churchill, the Labour party, led by Clement Attlee, won a victory in 1945.*

AND NOW — WIN THE PEACE

VOTE LABOUR

How Homes have Changed

Building new houses was a priority for the Labour government. After the war, there were huge shortages of timber and cement. New building materials and methods were needed to build the 1 million new homes the government had promised. One method was to make the parts of a house in a factory. Each piece could then be quickly assembled on site to make a prefabricated or 'prefab' home.

The Rise and Fall of the Tower Block

Another way of solving the housing shortage was to build high-rise tower blocks. Between 1945 and the early 1950s, 6,544 tower blocks were built. But by the mid 1960s, tower blocks had become increasingly unpopular to live in as residents complained that the lifts and the grounds were often vandalised. Councils returned to building more traditional semi-detached and detached houses and smaller blocks of flats.

INVESTIGATE

Price of houses from 1948 to 2000

Find out the average house price in your area. How does it compare to 1948?

Year	Average House Price
2000	£101,500
1995	£65,600
1990	£59,700
1985	£31,100
1980	£23,500
1975	£11,700
1970	£4,900
1965	£3,600
1960	£2,500
1955	£2,000
1950	£1,900
1948	£1,700

Source: National House Building Council

TIMELINE

1945–51	840,000 new houses are built but over 1.5 million are needed
1949	London's first ten-story council tower block opens in Holborn
1968	Ronan Point tower block collapses. Four people are killed and 17 injured
1980	The 1980 Housing Act gives tenants the right to buy the council houses they rent
2007	Some houses in England and Wales are given an energy efficiency rating

▲ **Prefabricated houses** • Prefabs were one answer to the housing shortage after the war. In the background it is possible to see some of the damage caused by the bombing raids.

Thames Gateway • *It is hoped that the London Olympics in 2012 will create huge opportunities to redevelop poorer parts of the city.*

Owning Your Own Home

In the 1980s, Margaret Thatcher's Conservative government announced that it wanted more people to own their own homes rather than renting them. It was believed that as homeowners, people would feel more responsible for keeping their homes in good condition. The 1980 Housing Act forced councils to give their tenants the 'right to buy' their council houses. By 1999, 68% of the houses in Britain were privately owned, compared to just 32% in 1953.

SOUNDBITES
The rising population created a huge demand for housing and building new homes is a major source of **employment**. In the 1970s, central heating and double-glazed windows were introduced, helping to make homes more energy-efficient.

Housing Problems in the Twenty First Century

While the standard of homes had improved vastly since the 1950s, new difficulties emerged. From the 1980s onwards, the cost of buying a house started to rise at a frightening pace. In 2007, the cost of an average house was almost seven times the average annual wage, making it difficult for young people to get on the 'property ladder'.

There is also an increased awareness about how we use our planet's energy resources. New homes being built need to run much more energy efficiently, with improved insulation and in some cases using **renewable energy sources**, such as solar power, for heating and electricity.

Looking After the Home

Just after the Second World War, many houses only had gas to supply all their lighting and cooking needs. Some houses even had very old-fashioned Victorian cast iron ranges to heat water and cook on. Appliances such as vacuum cleaners and washing machines were too expensive for many to buy.

Making Housework Easier

Things began to change in the 1950s. As wages began to increase, more families could buy electrical appliances that made housework easier. People now had vacuum cleaners and washing machines to do the jobs for them.

In the 1950s, twin-tub washing machines became popular, followed by automatic washing machines in the 1960s. By the end of the 1960s, one in two homes had a washing machine and today just about every home has one. Not only were electrical appliances becoming common, houses became more comfortable in other ways, too.

Voices from history

'You've no idea how cold it could get in our house during the winter. We only had a coal fire and when your bare feet touched the lino at the edges of the room you had to make a leap onto the hall carpet. We couldn't afford to have heating on in the rest of the house although if it got really bad then we put on the two bar electric fire in the bedroom but only until we were under the covers. In the morning we could draw patterns in the frost on the inside of the window.'

A member of the author's family speaking about life in a coal fired house on Tyneside, in the 1950s.

◀ **Electrical power in 1953** • *Most of the domestic appliances we have in our homes today had been invented before 1948. However, it wasn't until the 1950s that people could begin to afford them and companies began to heavily market them to the public.*

Here is new efficiency in cooking — the master cooker which will add beauty to your kitchen. See it at your Local Dealers or Electricity Showrooms.

G.E.C.
The name to remember for all electric appliances in the home

G.E.C. YOUR GUARANTEE

KINGSWAY LONDON WC2

Before the 1970s, some homes only had a single coal fire in the main room to heat the whole house. Other rooms would often be very cold during the winter. From the 1970s onwards, more and more homes had central heating. This helped to make the whole house much warmer and new types of boilers gave instant hot water. Double-glazed windows meant that houses could retain their heat better and insulation materials in walls and roof spaces also helped keep houses warmer.

Better Homes – but at a Price

By the twenty first century, homes had about 35 different electrical appliances, including fridges, washing machines, computers and DVD players. But their effect on our environment has become a public concern. In 1999, world leaders met in Kyoto, Japan to discuss these issues. Governments were encouraged to switch from traditional energy sources to renewable ones, such as wind and water power.

CHANGING TIMES

In the twenty first century, we depend on oil for 90% of our transport needs. It is also used in the development of chemicals and pharmaceuticals. Experts estimate that current oil reserves will only last for about 40 years.

▲
Electrical power today • *The range of electronic equipment in the home in the twenty first century is immense and it is set to grow even more.*

The use of long-life light bulbs and switching off household appliances rather than leaving them on 'standby' after use and during the night, are now encouraged and promoted by environmental groups who see these measures as ways of conserving energy in our homes.

Furnishing the Home

During the Second World War, many materials were in short supply. In 1941, the government introduced a range of basic furniture called *Standard Emergency Furniture*. This type of furniture was known as 'Utility' furniture. 'Utility' meant making do with the materials you had. The concept of 'do-it-yourself' or DIY began in the 1950s. It became cheaper to make home improvements by buying packs of ready-made materials and assembling them at home.

CHANGING TIMES

All wartime furniture had to be made to government specifications. If it did not, the makers could be imprisoned.

New Styles

After restrictions were lifted in 1948, families began to spend more money on furnishing their homes. Newer houses were often smaller so furniture needed to be compact.

Simple designs, influenced by the Scandinavian 'minimalist' style, became popular as they were very different from the old, heavy and ornate Victorian style that had been popular before the war.

Psychedelic

By the 1970s, a huge explosion of colour had taken place in the world of fashion. These psychedelic images influenced the colours people used to decorate their homes. Bright oranges, reds and purples were used as furniture colours and wall decorations. Brightly coloured plastics were also widely used, not only for furniture, but also for a whole range of household objects.

The psychedelic • Antique dealers buy and sell furniture from the 1970s for many times their original value. These 'lava' lamps were very popular in 'trendy' 1970s homes and are highly collectable today.

TIMELINE

1956	The Ideal Home Exhibition presents the 'House of the Future'
1958	The first electric power tool is produced for home improvers
1965	Haggerty Enterprises of Chicago market the Lava Lite Lamp
1987	The first IKEA store is opened in Britain
1996	The BBC televises the first episode of *Changing Rooms*, a popular home makeover series

SOUNDBITES

In the 1980s, as more people began to own their own homes, people wanted to improve them. DIY was an inexpensive way of doing this. The DIY industry also created jobs in DIY stores across Britain.

Minimalism • *This style of furniture is fashionable today. Its neutral colours are very different from the psychedelic furniture of the 1970s.*

Do-It-Yourself

By the late 1980s, Britain's economy had grown rapidly and people had more money to spend on their homes. The psychedelic style began to look old-fashioned. Black and white and soft pastels became the colours of choice for furnishings. For those who could not afford expensive furniture, huge stores and warehouses, such as IKEA, offered cheaper styles. They sold pre-assembly packs, offering everything from garden furniture to kitchen and bedroom units.

Incomes increased even further in the twenty first century and more people began taking out loans to fund their lifestyles. At the same time manufacturers were developing new methods for mass-producing goods relatively cheaply. Television companies quickly saw an opportunity with the rise in the popularity of DIY. Home improvement programmes such as *Changing Rooms* and *Groundforce* were televised for the first time in the 1990s and won large audiences.

Childhood

The twentieth century has sometimes been called the 'century of the child', as it was a time when the lives of many children improved in three ways: health, education and the right to fair treatment.

Medical Care

When the National Health Service (NHS) was introduced in 1948, special attention was paid to the health of children. The introduction of vaccinations and **immunisation** against common childhood illnesses, such as **polio** greatly reduced the number of infant deaths in Britain. Payments, called Family Allowances were made to parents, to help buy essential foods to ensure that their children were well-nourished.

*Toys at Christmas • A little girl sends a note up the chimney for Santa in the 1950s. Parents did not have a huge amount of **disposable income** so presents would have been much smaller and fewer than they are today.*

CHANGING TIMES

In 2006, from birth to leaving university at the age of 21 it cost parents on average more than £180,000 to feed, clothe and school their children.

Rising living standards in the 1950s, and smaller families meant that a family's resources were spread between fewer children. By the twenty first century, British parents were spending more on their children than any other country in Europe. Raising children has become so expensive that 12% of families seek help with costs from grandparents.

TIMELINE

1946	The introduction of Family Allowance
1948	The introduction of the National Health Service (NHS)
1969	The introduction of the Children and Young Persons Act
1982	Physical punishment in schools is banned
2004	The introduction of the Children Act

Electronic games • A family sit down to play games on a Playstation. The electronic games console is very popular in Britain today but it is quite expensive.

Healthier and Wealthier

Not only do more children survive into adulthood than they did in 1948, but they are taller and stronger, too. By the beginning of the twenty first century, children in many families could expect financial support into their twenties, something that would have been unimaginable in the early 1950s. In the 1950s, most children left school at the age of 14, found a job and contributed to the **family income**. In the late 1960s, the school leaving age was raised to 16. In the twenty first century, more young people than ever want to stay on at school and develop further skills by going to college or university.

More Rights for Children

Another change that happened from the 1970s onwards, was that children were given new rights. The Children and Young Persons Act of 1969 ensured that a young person who broke the law would not be taken into custody in an adult prison. Using physical punishment was banned in all schools in 1982 and by the 1990s, children's views were taken into account if their parents divorced.

INVESTIGATE | The average cost of bringing up one child

In the first 5 years	£46,695
Years 6-11	£31,000
Years 12-18	£33,747
Years 19-21	£30,000

Source: BBC News website

> **Why do you think the costs are greater from years 1–5 than 19–21?**

The Car

In 1948, the motor car was a luxury item that few families could afford. During the 1950s however, the country's **economy** was stronger and people were earning more so they could afford to buy a car. But cars in the 1950s were not very sophisticated. There were virtually no safety features and heating and car radios were looked upon as expensive 'extras'.

Car Style

In the 1960s, even more people could afford a car, and style became important. The Morris Mini-Minor was the fashionable car of the 1960s. It made its first appearance in 1959.

It was a revolutionary design, compact but spacious enough for four people. It has remained popular ever since, although it has been succeeded by newer versions, such as the Mini Clubman in 1969.

Benefits of the Car

Having a car altered families lifestyles considerably, making travel a far easier task. They could get to school and work, or take trips and holidays without having to rely on public transport.

THE REVOLUTIONARY "QUALITY FIRST" MORRIS MINI-MINOR

WIZARDRY ON WHEELS

PUBLICATION No. H. & E. 3050A

▲ **The Morris Mini-Minor** • *This car first came off the production line in 1959, and quickly became one of the symbols of 'swinging' Britain in the 1960s.*

TIMELINE

1948	The 'revolutionary' Morris Mini-Minor makes its appearance at the Earl's Court Motor Show
1959	The first Morris Mini-Minor rolls off the production line
1991	The wearing of seat belts in the front of cars becomes compulsory
1999	The Kyoto summit on global warming points to the growth in cars as a factor in global warming

The city • Streets in Britain's towns and cities are becoming very congested and there is little sign that the rise in road traffic is slowing down.

The Dangers of Cars

During the 1980s, concerns grew about the number of road casualties. In 1983, the government made it compulsory for all cars to be fitted with seat belts and for improved car designs to protect passengers in the event of an accident. Electronic equipment such as electronic windows and CD players, have also become popular features, turning the car into more than a practical means of transport.

Problems with Cars

In the twenty first century there are many families who have two or more cars. In fact, there are ten times more cars on the road compared to the 1950s. The maintenance of existing roads and motorways and the construction of new roads barely keeps pace with the increasing numbers of cars.

Some cities, like London, have introduced congestion charges to reduce the number of cars coming into city centres to allow traffic to flow more freely.

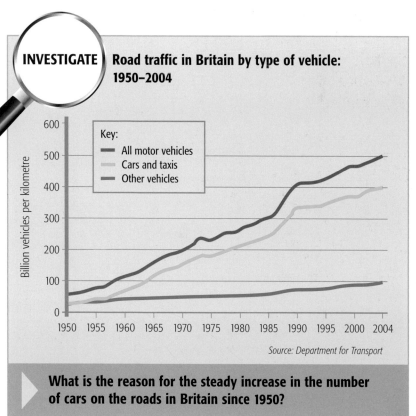

INVESTIGATE **Road traffic in Britain by type of vehicle: 1950–2004**

Key:
- All motor vehicles
- Cars and taxis
- Other vehicles

Billion vehicles per kilometre

Source: Department for Transport

What is the reason for the steady increase in the number of cars on the roads in Britain since 1950?

17

Radio and Television

The first television programmes began in 1936. Television sets were bulky and expensive, with tiny screens. Only about 20,000 people in London had television sets and when the Second World War broke out, all television programmes were suspended. Choice was limited after the war, as only the BBC was broadcasting in 1948.

The Wireless

In the late 1940s and early 1950s, families often listened to the 'wireless'. Unlike most other countries, Britain had an independent broadcasting system, the British Broadcasting Corporation (BBC), which was paid for from viewers and listeners' licence fees and not from advertising.

By 1960, television was taking over from the wireless. A staggering 25 million people saw the coronation of Queen Elizabeth II in 1953 on the television.

Television Takes Over

In 1955 a new channel, ITV, was launched, paid for by advertising revenue rather than a licence fee. Other channels followed; BBC 2 in 1964 and Channel 4 in 1982. All programmes were in black and white until 1967, when colour was first introduced. The launching of the *Telstar* satellite in 1962, when pictures were beamed across the Atlantic, opened up vast possibilities for communication. The *Telstar* satellite was used to send information about the assassination of the American President, John F Kennedy in 1963, across the Atlantic to Britain – and then to feed back the reactions from Europe to America.

CHANGING TIMES

On Sunday, during the 1950s, there would be a two hour break in programmes on the television so people could go to church.

A Digital Era

By the late 1960s and early 1970s, video recorders and later, in the 1990s, DVD players, meant families could record their favourite programmes and watch them whenever they wanted to. In the twenty first century, technology has advanced to the point where large flat screen televisions with better picture quality have been developed. With higher incomes and more loans available today, an increasing number of people have been able to afford them. In the late 1990s, digital television was introduced, increasing the opportunities for even more television channels. In 2007, High Definition Television (HDTV) was made widely accessible to most of the UK and created the possibility for even more channels.

TIMELINE

1953	The coronation of Queen Elizabeth II is shown on television
1955	Commercial television begins – ITV
1967	Colour television starts
1978	The first home video recorder goes on sale
2007	High Definition Television (HDTV) is launched

▲

The wireless • The radio was a popular form of entertainment in the 1940s and 1950s. Today we have much more choice, from televisions and DVDs to MP3 Players and video games.

Television, like the radio or the 'wireless', has been important in influencing people's opinions. It has visually brought the news into the homes of people across Britain and television programmes on social issues, such as *Jamie's School Dinners,* have made governments take action. Presenters and programmes reflect a diversity of cultures, that means television has played an important role in celebrating Britain as a multicultural country.

Voices from history

There are worries that people's health might be damaged by the amount of television people watch today:

'The average six-year-old child in Britain will have spent one full year watching television and over half of three-year-olds have a TV set in their bedroom.'

Dr Aric Sigman voicing concerns about television viewing on children's health in an article for the Manchester Evening News.

The Cinema

Before television, the cinema was one of the most popular forms of family entertainment. Many people went once or twice a week to watch a film. For as little as 6 pence you could watch the news, a short film and the feature film all in one viewing.

At its Height

In 1948, there were 4,700 cinemas in Britain, with about 30 million people going each week. Many films were made in Hollywood in America but the government helped to make British films popular too by providing funding. Hollywood films were usually lavish productions, while British films were often made on a smaller scale and budget.

SOUNDBITES

Technology is used to create thrilling special effects in films and TV programmes. Film and cinema entertainment is now a global industry.

ET • Made in 1982, ET used special effects to capture audiences and became one of the best-loved children's films of the 1980s.

TIMELINE

1940s	Cinema is the most popular form of mass entertainment
1953	The first film in wide screen Cinemascope, *The Robe*, is released to try and win back audiences
1985	The first multiplex cinema with many screens opens in Milton Keynes
2006	The first Nintendo Wii games console goes on sale

Cinemas in Decline

All this was to change. By 1968, the number of cinemas had shrunk to 2,000 and audiences to just 2 million. The cause of this change was, of course, access to television, which offered cheap and enjoyable entertainment at home, for all the family every night of the week.

Fighting Back

At first the film industry fought back with famous film stars, such as Charlton Heston and Elizabeth Taylor in spectacular films such as *Ben Hur* and *Cleopatra*. But these efforts failed to win back steady audiences to the cinema. The growth of the video recorder from the late 1970s and DVD players from the early 1990s onwards, was a further blow to cinemas. Viewers could now buy a copy of their favourite programmes and films to watch whenever they wanted to.

The Cinema Makes a Comeback

By the late 1980s, it looked as though cinemas would not survive the competition from videos and DVDs. But the cinema industry responded by creating multi-screen cinemas that could show many different films at the same time, within the same cinema building.

INVESTIGATE Average weekly cinema attendance from 1946 to 2006

	Millions	Year	Millions
1946	1,635.0	1978	126.1
1948	1,514.0	1980	101.0
1950	1,395.8	1982	64.0
1952	1,312.1	1984	54.0
1954	1,275.8	1986	75.5
1956	1,100.8	1988	84.0
1958	754.7	1990	97.37
1960	500.8	1992	103.64
1962	395.0	1994	123.53
1964	342.8	1996	123.8
1966	288.8	1998	135.5
1968	237.3	2000	142.5
1970	193.0	2002	175.9
1972	156.6	2004	171.2
1974	138.5	2006	156.6
1976	103.9		

Source: Dodana 2005

> When were cinema audiences at their lowest? Attendance in 2006 is still below that of the 1940s and 1950s. How have cinemas managed to survive?

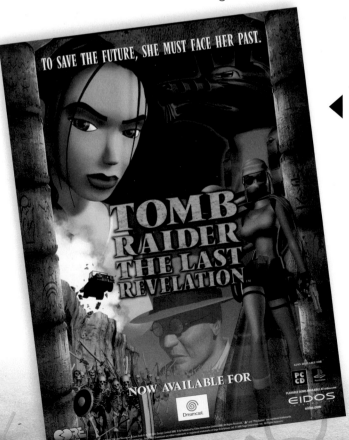

Money beyond the film • *The toys and games based on the characters in films are very profitable for film makers. Electronic computer games such as this Playstation game are amongst the most popular.*

In the twenty first century, computer-generated technology is expensive but it means films such as *Shrek* and *Beowulf* can be created entirely by computer animation. The film companies quickly realised that they could increase their profits and advertise their films by producing toys and games. In doing so films today can make money in an era where film-going is not as popular as it was in 1948.

Family Holidays

In the 1950s, seaside resorts such as Great Yarmouth, Brighton and Blackpool were the most popular holiday destinations for many British families. Holidaymakers with money to spend could stay in hotels, while less well-off families often stayed in guest houses.

Butlin's

Some families preferred to go to the increasingly popular holiday camps, first opened by Billy Butlin in the 1930s. A week's stay for a family at a holiday camp cost about a week's wages, and all entertainment facilities were provided.

The 'Package' Holiday

As people began to earn more money in the late 1950s and early 1960s, some preferred to go abroad where they could experience other cultures and visit new places.

Travel companies began to organise 'package' holidays, booking the flight and hotel for a group of travellers. The most popular destination for British tourists was Spain, where food and drink were cheap.

Butlin's holiday camp • *Butlin's holiday camps were very popular in the 1950s, providing plenty of entertainment for all the family at a price most people could afford.*

TIMELINE

1940s	Most families have holidays in Britain. The seaside was the most popular location
1950s	Butlin's holiday camps become a favourite holiday destination for families
1979	2.5 million Britons go on 'package' holidays
1995	Easyjet, one of the first budget airlines, offers cheap flights across Europe

▲
Air travel • *With cheaper air travel it is now possible to visit places, such as Crete, which would have been difficult to go to forty years ago.*

CHANGING TIMES

Climate change may lead to the British package holiday to the Mediterranean becoming a thing of the past. Places like Majorca may be too hot by 2030, and will have to be replaced by cooler UK holidays.

Holidaying abroad has become more and more popular. By the 1980s, air fares were cheaper and some families holidayed in destinations thousands of miles away, such as Disney World in Florida. Foreign holidays had become a normal part of family life rather than a privilege that only the well-off could afford.

Cheap Travel

Today, many people arrange their holiday on the internet. Cheaper travel, however, has meant more journeys are made using aircraft. This has caused more pollution and environmental damage as new airports and runways are built. However, never has the opportunity for the majority of people to travel and learn about other countries been greater.

Changes in Food

In the 1950s, few homes had fridges. Along with food shortages and tight budgets it was usual for people to shop daily. Most of this shopping was done in local stores along the main street of towns. Each shop specialised in selling one type of **commodity**, so people would visit separate shops to buy meat, vegetables and bread.

Food in Season

There was much less choice in the 1950s. **Rationing** was still in place in the early 1950s so there was a limit to the quantity of each item one person could purchase. Fresh fruit and vegetables were bought mainly from British growers, so people ate what was in season. Shoppers queued at the counter, and took home what was in stock.

Voices from history

'When my parents first came to settle in Britain I didn't like the food at school. It seemed very stodgy and boring and I much preferred food at home. My mum used a lot of herbs and spices and this made things very tasty. My friends used to ask if they could come home with me because they liked my mum's cooking. '

Memories of an Italian child who came to live in Britain in 1965.

▲
1950 grocery store • *All the goods were stacked on and behind the counter and customers had to wait their turn to be served.*

TIMELINE

1954	Rationing ends
1969	The first Indian takeaway opens in Leeds
1982	*An Invitation to Indian Cooking* first airs on the BBC
1993	Sainsbury's product range rises from 7,000 items in 1980, to 17,000 items in 1993
2006	The government's healthy eating campaign to 'eat five portions a day', means more people are buying fruit and vegetables than ever before

Rise of the Supermarket

Food shopping was transformed in the late 1950s. Bigger food retailers began to open self-service shops or supermarkets, an idea that had originated in America. They offered a range of pre-packed frozen meals, alongside other food products.

As more and more families began to own cars, supermarkets became larger and were usually built on the outskirts of towns. They sold a whole range of household goods. This meant many smaller shops could not match supermarket prices, so they went out of business. It is now also possible to order goods online and have them delivered to the door.

New Foods

By the twenty first century, the range and types of food people ate had increased enormously. This was partly the result of immigration from Asia, the West Indies and, more recently, other parts of the **European Union**. Improved transport meant that fresh food could be flown or shipped in from all over of the world. Restaurants and takeaways introduced food from many different cultures and countries, such as China and India. Eating became a social occasion, with more people eating out.

The Big 4 · *The four biggest supermarkets (Tesco, Sainsbury's, Asda and Morrisons – known as the 'Big 4') had a combined share of 75.63% of the UK grocery market in 2007.*

Shops and Shopping

Even though rationing on clothes had been lifted by 1950, the choice of different types of clothing was still very limited. This was because there were still shortages of materials several years after the war had ended.

The Standard of Living

However in the 1950s, families had more money coming in and more disposable income to spend. They wanted to improve the quality of their lives and began to buy a greater variety of goods. People began to spend more money on luxury items such as holidays, cars and clothes for all of the family in the latest fashions and styles.

1950s boutique • A shop assistant shows a dress to a customer in a women's clothing boutique. ▶

Shopping Centres

In the 1970s and 1980s, as town centres were redeveloped, shopping centres began to be built. Based on the American-style shopping mall, they contained restaurants, coffee shops, banks and building societies and cinemas. Chains of shops became popular in shopping centres and towns all over the country. These 'chains' could sell products more cheaply on a mass scale.

TIMELINE

1949	Clothes rationing ends
1964	Topshop established in the department store, Peter Robinson, in Sheffield
1975	Sainsbury's opens the first hypermarket. It offers consumer goods as well as food ranges
2007	£1 out of every £8 spent is spent at Tesco

From the 1990s, shopping centres, such as Bluewater in Kent and the Trafford Centre near Manchester, were increasingly built on the edges of towns and cities where they could be reached by car. Families could park easily and visit many shops at once. Shopping became a social occasion, where families could combine a trip to the shops with eating out at a restaurant and going to see a film at the cinema.

Chains • *In high streets and malls the small, independent shop has been replaced by 'chains', such as Burton. How many chain shops can you see in this photo?*

SOUNDBITES

Changes in technology have produced new ways of buying and making goods. Today, people can choose to shop using the internet, through websites such as Amazon and ebay.

Clothes become Cheaper

Today, society is a **consumer society** where many people spend a lot of money on the latest clothing fashions. In the twenty first century, large stores and supermarkets such as Primark and Asda, sell clothes at very competitive prices. In November 2007, Primark announced profits of more than £600 million.

A Multicultural Society

British families have changed enormously since 1948. In the late 1940s and 1950s, most families were white and Christian. Today Britain is a multi-ethnic country with immigrant families from many different cultural backgrounds, practising many different religions. Although all British citizens obey the same laws, it is accepted that different cultural groups have the right to express their own ideas and beliefs, as long as they do not break the law.

The new Britain • *After the Second World War people from* **Commonwealth** *countries were invited to 'the motherland' to make up the shortfall of workers needed to rebuild war-torn Britain.*

Racial Prejudice

This ethnic diversity was not achieved without some difficulty. Immigrant families often got the worst housing in the old areas of the inner cities.

TIMELINE

1948	Arrival of the ship the *Empire Windrush* with immigrants from the West Indies	
1958	Race riots in the Notting Hill area of London over inequalities for black people	
1965	The introduction of the Race Relations Act	
1965	The first Notting Hill Carnival takes place	
1976	The introduction of the Racial Equality Act	
2001	Race riots in Bradford	

Sometimes families were **discriminated** against. This may have been because of the colour of their skin or the religion they practice. The government wanted to see that the new immigrants were treated fairly and so the Race Relations Act was passed in 1965, followed by the Racial Equality Act in 1976. These laws made it illegal to discriminate against minority people in housing as well as work. New laws, however, did not always solve discrimination and in some cities, riots occurred in areas where there was a concentration of minority ethnic groups.

People from different cultures have made an enormous contribution to the richness of life in this country. Not only have they changed the foods we eat, but also the clothes we wear, the music we listen to and the art we enjoy. Quite often this has taken the form of a mixing of cultures, such as pop/bhangra, and festivals such as Mela and Notting Hill. British families practise a range of religions today, including Hinduism and Islam and mosques and temples stand alongside Christian churches.

More recently, immigrants have come from Eastern European countries which have become members of the European Community. The European Community allows its members to travel to other parts of the European Union to search for work and many immigrant workers have come to Britain.

Arriving in their thousands • Since Poland joined the European Union in 2004, over 600,000 Poles have come to Britain.

▼

Timeline *Highlights in the History of Britain since 1948*

1948 Labour government introduces the National Health Service (NHS)

1948 The arrival of immigrants aboard the *Empire Windrush*

1953 The televising of the coronation of Queen Elizabeth II

1954 Rationing ends

1955 Commercial television begins – ITV

1956 The Ideal Home Exhibition presents the 'House of the Future'

1958 Race riots in Notting Hill

1959 The first Morris Mini-Minor car comes of the production line

1960 The contraceptive pill goes on sale in Britain

1965 The introduction of the Race Relations Act

1968 Ronan Point tower block collapses, four people are killed and 17 are injured

1967 First colour TV transmissions

1969 The introduction of the Children and Young Persons Act

1970 The Equal Pay Act – women receive the same wage as men for the same job

1976 The introduction of the Race Relations Act

1978 The first home video recorder goes on sale

1980 The Housing Act gives tenants the right to buy the council houses they rent

1982 Physical punishment is banned in state schools

1983 The wearing of seat belts becomes law

1995 Easyjet, one of the first budget airlines, offers cheap flights across Europe

1996 BBC televises the first episode of the DIY programme *Changing Rooms*

1999 Kyoto Summit on global warming

1999 The first DVD recorder goes on sale

2001 Race riots in Bradford

2004 Same sex couples are permitted to marry under the Civil Partnerships Act

2004 The introduction of the Children Act

2006 The first Nintendo Wii games console goes on sale

2007 £1 out of every £8 spent is spent at Tesco

2007 House prices fall in many parts of the country. This makes it easier for young people to buy their own home

Glossary

commodity A natural product that can be bought and sold

Commonwealth Association of countries once in the British Empire

consumer society When we are encouraged to buy as much as we can. This creates more jobs and everyone becomes better off

discrimination The unfair treatment of a person

disposable income Money that is left from someone's wages once rent, bills and food have been paid for

divorce Going to court to legally end a marriage

economy A system in which a country organises the production of goods and services, their distribution and their sale

employment A person's work or profession

European Union An alliance between certain countries in Europe

family income The total of all the money coming into in a household during the year

flea A small insect that feeds on the blood of humans and animals

immunisation To protect people against a disease, often by inoculation

inoculation To introduce a mild form of infection into the body so that the body builds up a resistance

measles An infectious viral disease causing fever and a red rash, typically occurring in childhood

polio A virus that attacks the nervous system. It can cause total paralysis in a matter of hours and can strike at any age, but mainly affects children younger than three-years-old

psychedelic Music, culture or art from the 1970s

rationing Sharing out food and goods equally so that no one goes without

renewable energy source A type of energy that can be used again and again, for example wind and water

scabies A skin disease caused by a mite infection. Symptons are itching and small, raised red spots

two-up, two-down A standard working class house with two bedrooms on the first floor and two rooms on the ground floor

vaccination To inoculate a person with a mild form of one disease to protect them from another, for example to inoculate with cowpox to prevent smallpox

whooping cough An infectious bacterial disease affecting children. One of the main symptoms is a convulsive cough followed by a whoop

FURTHER INFORMATION

📖 Books

Britain Since World War II: Home Life
Stewart Ross
(Franklin Watts, 2007)

Explore History: Britain Since 1930
Jane Shuter
(Heinemann Library, 2005)

Britain Since World War II: Health and Diet
Stewart Ross
(Franklin Watts, 2007)

🖱 Websites

http://www.museumoflondon.org.uk/archive/exhibits/festival/
Look back at the spectacular Festival of Britain

http://www.connectedearth.com/LearningCentre/HowhaslifeinBritainchanged/index.htm
Look at many different aspects of life since 1948 and how home life has changed since the Second World War

http://www.movinghere.org.uk/
You can research 200 years of migration in England

Index

air travel 23, **23**
Attlee, Clement 5

BBC 18
birth control 13
bombing raids 4, 6
Butlin's holiday camps 22, **22**

cars 16–17, **17**, 25, 27
childhood 14–15
Churchill, Winston 5
cinema 20–21, 27
climate change 9, 23
clothes 26, 27, 29
Conservative government 7
council houses 5, 6, 7

digital television 18
diseases 5, 14
divorce 12, 13, 15
'do-it-yourself' (DIY) 10, 11
DVDs 18, 21

economy 11, 16
education 12, 13, 15
electrical appliances 8, 9, **9**
employment 7, 11, 12
energy 7, 9
European Union 25, 29

family life 12–13
films 20–21
food 5, 14, 24–25, 29
fridges 8, 24
furniture 10–11

health care 5, 14
heating 7, 8, 9
holidays 16, 22–23
houses
    building 6–7
    electrical appliances 8, 9
    furnishing 10–11
    heating 7, 8, 9
    ownership 7
    prices 6, 7
    slums 4–5
housework 8, 13

immigration 25, 28–29
income 11, 13, 15
inoculation 5

Labour government 4, 5

manufacturing industry 11, 27
marriage 12, 13
measles 5
multicultural society 19, 28–29, **28**

National Health Service (NHS) 5, 14

'package' holidays 22
polio 14
pollution 23
population growth 7
poverty 5
prefabs 6, **6**
psychedelic style 10, 11

radio 18, 19, **19**
rationing 24, 26
refrigerators 8, 24
religions 28, 29
renewable energy 7, 9
riots 28
road traffic 16–17

satellites 18
Second World War 4, 18
shopping 24–25, **24**, 26–27, **26–27**
supermarkets 25

television 11, 18–19, 20
Telstar satellite 18
Thatcher, Margaret 7
tourism 22–23
tower blocks 6
travel
    cars 16–17
    holidays 22–23
'two-up, two-down' houses 4, 30

university 12, 15
'Utility' furniture 10

vaccination 5, 14, 30
vacuum cleaners 8
videos 18, 21

washing machines 8
whooping cough 5, 30
wireless 18, 19, **19**
women 12, 13

The numbers in **bold** type refer to an illustration.